Language on the Move >>

Italian

The perfect language course for the savvy traveler

Published by Hinkler Books Pty Ltd
45–55 Fairchild Street
Heatherton Victoria 3202 Australia
www.hinkler.com.au

hinkler

© Hinkler Books Pty Ltd 2009, 2015

Writer: Sue Farley
Translator: Dörte Horn
Italian voice: Luciana Tiresen
English voice: Ross Newth
Editors: Louise Coulthard and Suzannah Pearce
Art direction and internal design: Michael Raz
CD and multimedia design and production: www.proeye.tv
Recorded at Abe's Audio (Tasmania, Australia)

Images © Shutterstock.com: Colosseum in Rome © Filipe Frazao;
Ancona © onairda; Cheese market © Artens; Venice carnival © Mario
Maganto Berdejo; Gondolas at The Grand Canal © Mila Atkovska;
Campanile Giotto, Florence, Italy © saras66; Statue of David ©
Brandon Bourdages; Typical old street © Claudio Giovanni Colombo;
Pasta with fish ragout © marco mayer.

ISBN: 978 1 4889 2675 4

Printed and bound in China

Language on the Move »

Italian

The perfect language course for the savvy traveler

hinkler

> Contents

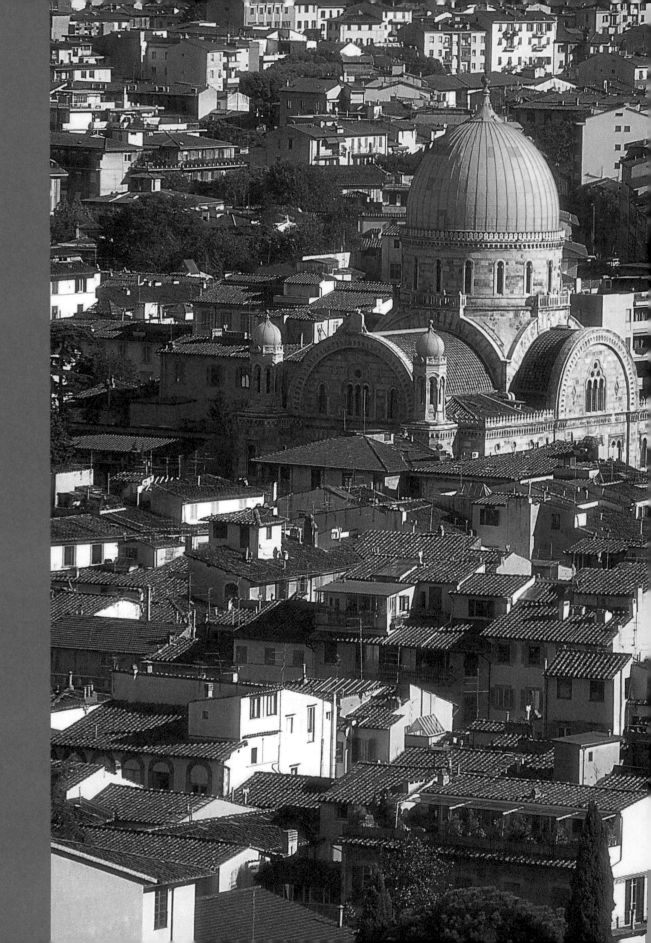

Introduction

> Introduction

Traveling through Italy is wonderful – the food, the art, the tiny sidewalk cafés, the noisy piazzas, frantic city streets, and quiet hillside villages. There are the ancient ruins in Rome and the sun-soaked beaches of the Amalfi Coast to explore; the fabulous wines of Tuscany and chances to wander through national parks. There are new sights and sounds at every corner and new adventures at every crossroads.

Whether you're traveling for pleasure, business, or a little of both, speaking some of the language is the key to successful everyday interaction with others. In many parts of Italy, the local people will have very little, if any, English, so it's up to you to cross the language barrier and use the local lingo. Locals generally admire anyone who attempts to use their beautiful language, no matter how bad it sounds at first. They see it as a mark of respect that you, a traveler to their country, have put in the time and effort to become familiar with their language.

If you master the basics before you travel things will be a lot easier. Although, to the beginner, the Italian of native speakers won't sound at all like the carefully worded phrases you learned before you arrived, just ask the person you're speaking with to slow down, and explain that you have very little Italian. They'll appreciate your honesty and will usually be more than happy to accommodate you. These words and phrases will help you get started:

ENGLISH	ITALIAN	PRONUNCIATION
Do you speak English?	Parli Inglese?	par-lee Een-gli-si
A little.	Un poco.	un po-ko
Do you speak Italian?	Parli Italiano?	par-lee Eeta-lea-no
I only speak a little Italian.	Solo un poco.	so-lo un po-ko
What is this called in Italian?	Come si chiama questo in Italiano?	ko-me see ke-a-ma kwe-sto een Eeta-lea-no
I'm sorry. I don't understand.	Mi spiace, ma non capisco.	me spee-achey, ma non ka-pee-sko
Please speak more slowly.	Può parlare lentamente per piacere.	può par-la-re len-ta-men-ti per pea-che-rey
Could you say that again, please?	Può ripetere per piacere?	può ree-pe-te-re per pea-che-rey

You'll also need a few courtesy phrases, like 'hello' and 'goodbye', 'please' and 'thank you'.

Hello	Ciao	chow
Good morning	Buongiorno	buon-geor-no
Goodbye	Arrivederci	ar-ree-vee-dir-chee
Please	Per piacere	per pea-che-rey
Thank you	Grazie	gra-zea
Excuse me	Mi scusi	me sku-see
Yes	Si	see
No	No	no
Sorry	Mi spiace	me speea-che
Okay	Okay	okay

Through this *Language on the Move* phrasebook, the series of five CDs, and the accompanying multimedia DVD, we'll work to make a range of everyday interactions easier and more understandable, and bring you some local color and flavor along the way as well.

This first chapter and CD cover the basic aspects of conversation – things like the use of gender with nouns, how to pronounce the sounds, and some useful words and phrases for your first few hours on the ground, including money, time, directions, and numbers.

The second chapter and CD move on to travel essentials – the words and phrases you'll need for asking more involved directions, checking into your hotel, enquiring how to catch the right train, producing the correct travel documents, and finding medical help.

The third chapter and CD cover the all-important topics of food and eating out – how to buy food at a market, order food and drinks at a restaurant, explain that you have food allergies or don't eat certain foods, and find out what local coffees are called and what the best local foods and wines are in a region.

The fourth chapter and CD delve into entertainment, offering phrases that will help you visit an art gallery, go shopping, and rent a bicycle. We'll look for places playing live music, find a nightclub, and catch a movie.

The fifth chapter and CD look at the language in a little more detail, discussing the basics of Italian grammar and providing some of the phrases that will be important if you're planning to spend a longer time in Italy.

Our multimedia DVD incorporates all the material in the CDs in MP3 files for downloading to your MP3 player or smartphone, and provides a video that will bring the learning experience to life with animated text.

All the information in this book is contained on the accompanying disks, with the Italian language sections spoken by a native speaker. The disks also contain bonus material; wherever you see the 'Bonus' icon in this book it indicates that there are longer, more detailed conversations on the CDs and DVD.

BONUS   Listen to the CDs or watch the DVD for extra material whenever you see this icon.

By the end of this series, you'll have a strong grasp of basic Italian and will be confident about tackling the busiest city and the most remote rural village – maybe not with the panache of the locals, but well enough to get you through in good shape.

So let's get started! First things first: we'll begin with the pronunciation.

Pronunciation

The Italian language uses the same basic alphabet as in English, and many of the letters are pronounced the same way. But there are differences, and pronunciation of some consonants differs depending on what letter precedes them. For example:

The letter 'c', if used before 'e' or 'i', is said 'ch', as in *cestino*.

- Before 'a', 'o' or 'u', it's a 'k' sound, as in *caffè*.
- The letters 'ch' together are also pronounced as 'k', as in *chiesa*.

The letter 'g' works in a similar way:

- If it comes before the letters 'e' or 'i', it has a soft sound, as in *gelato*.
- Before 'a', 'o', 'u' or 'h', it has a hard sound, as in *guida*.
- If 'g' comes before an 'l', it is pronounced 'lya' as in *tovaglia,* so it effectively becomes a silent letter.

The letter 'h' is always silent. The 'r' is rolled along the tongue, as in *riposare*. The double 'rr' is rolled even more strongly, as in *corriere*. And lastly, the letter 's' is usually spoken as it is in English, but if 's' is followed by a 'c', there are two different pronunciations. Before 'e' or 'i', 'sc' is pronounced softly as 'sh', as in *sciare*. In front of other vowels, it has a hard 'k' sound, as in *scarponi*.

In general, the vowel sounds of Italian are shorter than they are in English, although most do have a longer form.

The nouns

Every noun in Italian is either masculine or feminine, which is shown by the different forms of the Italian equivalent of 'the' and 'a'. *Il* and *un* are the masculine versions; *la* and *una* are the feminine forms. Masculine nouns usually end in 'o', while feminine nouns usually end in 'a'. Nouns ending in 'e' can be either gender.

To say 'a market' or 'a beach' (that is, using the indefinite article instead of the definite), you use *un* or *una,* as in *un mercato* (masculine) and *una speeaggia* (feminine). The only time this changes is when the noun begins with a vowel or the letter combinations 'gn', 'sc', 'sp', 'st', or 'z', when it is always preceded by *uno*.

If you want to use the definite article, 'the', then 'the market' is *il mercato,* whereas 'the beach' is *la spiaggia*. Masculine nouns that begin with a vowel, or the letter combinations 'gn', 'sc', 'sp', 'st', or 'z', are preceded by *lo,* as in *lo zucchero* (the sugar).

Plurals of masculine nouns are preceded by the word *i* and the last letter is usually changed to 'i', as in *i mercati*. Plurals of feminine nouns are preceded by *le* and the last letter usually changes to 'e', as in *le spiagge*.

Adjectives in Italian must take on the gender of the noun they are describing. Usually, this is done by adding 'a' to the end of a feminine adjective and 'o' to the end of a masculine adjective. So you get *il mare azzurro* (the blue sea) and *la sciarpa nera* (the black scarf). As well as matching the gender of the noun they describe, adjectives match the number of the noun (that is, singular or plural). Masculine adjectives are made plural by adding an 'i' to the end (as in *i mari azzurri*), while feminine ones take an 'e' (as in *le sciarpe nere*). For adjectives ending in 'e', the plural form ends in 'i', as in *le scarpe verdi* (the green shoes).

Numbers

The numbers from one to twenty are as follows:

one	uno	uno
two	due	dua
three	tre	tre
four	quattro	kwat-tro
five	cinque	chin-kwe
six	sei	sei
seven	sette	set-teh
eight	otto	ot-to
nine	nove	no-vi
ten	dieci	dee-a-che
eleven	undici	un-dee-che
twelve	dodici	du-dee-che
thirteen	tredici	tre-dee-che
fourteen	quattordici	kwat-tor-dee-che
fifteen	quindici	kwin-dee-che
sixteen	sedici	se-dee-che
seventeen	diciassette	de-chias-set-teh
eighteen	diciotto	de-chiot-to
nineteen	diciannove	de-chan-no-ve
twenty	venti	ven-tee

The numbers from twenty to twenty-nine are expressed as the word for 'twenty' plus the word for 'one', then 'twenty' plus 'two', 'twenty' plus 'three', and so on.

twenty-one	ventuno	vin-tu-no
twenty-two	ventidue	vin-te-dua
twenty-three	ventitrè	vin-te-trì
twenty-four	ventiquattro	vin-te-kwat-tro
twenty-five	venticinque	vin-te-chin-kwe
twenty-six	ventisei	vin-te-sei
twenty-seven	ventisette	vin-te-sit-ti
twenty-eight	ventotto	vin-tot-to
twenty-nine	ventinove	vin-te-no-vi

All the numbers up to ninety-nine follow the same pattern, so you only need to learn the names of the multiples of ten, which are as follows:

thirty	trenta	tren-ta
forty	quaranta	kwa-ran-ta
fifty	cinquanta	chin-kwan-ta
sixty	sessanta	ses-san-ta

seventy	settanta	set-tan-ta
eighty	ottanta	ot-tan-ta
ninety	novanta	no-van-ta

thirty-one	trentuno	tren-tu-no
forty-five	quarantacinque	kwa-ran-ta-chin-kwe
fifty-eight	cinquantotto	chin-kwan-tot-to
sixty-seven	sessantasette	ses-san-ta-set-te
ninety-nine	novantanove	no-van-ta-no-ve

Above ninety-nine, the main numbers you need to know are:

one hundred	cento	chento
one thousand	mille	mil-le
one million	un milione	un me-leo-ne

You'll also need to know the names of a couple of common fractions:

a half	metà	me-tà
a quarter	un quarto	un kwar-to

Measurements and distances are given in metric units in Italian. Weight is measured in grams and kilograms; distance is measured in meters and kilometers; liquids are measured in milliliters and liters; and temperatures are expressed in degrees Celsius. A good guidebook will give you the conversions for these measurements in other systems.

Money

In Italy, the basic currency is the euro (€). There are a hundred euro cents in a euro, and coins come in €2, €1, 50¢, 20¢, 10¢, 5¢, 2¢, and 1¢ denominations. Euro notes come in €5, €10, €20, €50, €100, €200, and €500 denominations.

Money can be exchanged at many post offices and banks in Italy, and at some travel agencies and hotels. ATMs or cash machines can dispense cash if your card is compatible.

When you need to exchange money or get cash, here are some phrases you may need to know:

Where's the nearest bank?	Dov' è la banca più vicina?	dov-ay la ban-ka pew vee-cee-nah
Where's an ATM?	Dov' è un bancomat?	dov-ay un ban-co-mat
Can I change my traveler's checks here?	Posso cambiare i miei traveler's cheques qui?	posso kam-bee-arey e me-ai traveler's cheques kwi
Can I get cash out on my debit card?	Posso prelevare contanti con la mia carta bancomat?	poss-oh preh-leh-va-rey kon-tan-te kon la mia karta ban-ko-mat
Can I get cash out on my credit card here?	Posso prelevare contanti con la mia carta di credito?	poss-oh preh-leh-va-rey kon-tan-te kon la mea kar-ta dee cre-de-to?
What credit cards do you accept?	Che carte di credito acetate?	ke kar-te dee kre-de-to ac-chet-ta-teh
I'd like to exchange some money, please.	Vorrei cambiare un pò di soldi, per favore.	vor-rei kam-bea-re oon pò dee sol-de, per fa-vo-rey
I need €100 in smaller bills, please.	Ho bisogno di €100 in banconote di piccolo taglio, per favore.	ho bee-so-neo dee €100 en ban-co-no-ti dee peek-ko-lo ta-leo, per fa-vo-rey
Can I have some coins, please?	Posso avere della moneta per favore?	pos-so ave-rey del-la mo-ne-ta, per fa-vo-rey

Time

In Italian, time is expressed in hours – *le ore* – and minutes – *i minuti*. The twenty-four-hour clock is generally used for timetables and schedules, but people use the twelve-hour clock during everyday conversation, and specify the time of day with *di mattina* (morning), *di pomeriggio* (afternoon), and *di notte* (evening).

Here are the basic phrases you'll need:

What's the time, please?	Che ore sono, per piacere?	ke orey so-no per pea-che-rey
Right now it's (half past two).	Sono le (due e mezza).	sono li dua ey mez-za
Is it (4pm) yet?	Sono già le quattro?	so-no gea li kwattro
The next (train) leaves at (half past three) this afternoon.	Il prossimo treno parte alle (tre e mezza) questo pomeriggio.	el pros-see-mo tre-no par-te al-li tre ey mez-za kwe-sto po-me-reeg-geo
Our plane leaves at (a quarter to six) this evening.	Il nostro aereoplano parte alle (cinque e quarantacinque).	el nos-tro aero-pla-no par-tey al-li chin-kwe ey kwa-ran-ta-chin-kwe
The next bus is at (12.25pm).	Il prossimo bus è alle 12.25pm.	el pros-see-mo bus ey al-li 12.25pm
We have to wait for (two hours).	Dobbiamo aspettare per due ore.	dob-bia-mo asp-eh-ta-rey per dua orey
You can't check in until (three o'clock), which is an hour away.	Non puoi fare il check-in fino alle (tre), cioè fra un'ora.	non puo-ee fa-rey il check-in fee-no al-li tre, choe fra oon oray
The restaurant is open till (midnight).	Il ristorante è aperto fino a (mezzanotte).	el ree-sto-ran-tey ey aper-to fe-no a mez-za-not-tey
We'll meet here again at (midday).	Ci incontreremo qui di nuovo a mezzogiorno.	chee en-con-tre-rem-o kwi dee nuo-vo a mez-zo-geor-no

On your arrival in Italy, there are a few more phrases that will help you get smoothly through border control and to your accommodation:

You'll need your passport to get through immigration.	Serve il passaporto per il controllo passaporti.	ser-vey eel pas-sa-por-to per eel kon-trol-lo pas-sa-pot-rtee
Do you have a visa?	Hai un visto?	hae un vee-sto
Where's the customs desk, please?	Dov'è la dogana, per piacere?	dov-ay la do-ga-na, per pea-che-rey
Do you have anything to declare?	Niente da dichiarare?	nien-teh da dee-kea-ra-rey
Where have you come from today?	Da dove arriva?	da do-vey ar-ree-va
Where do I pick up my luggage?	Dove posso ritirare il mio bagaglio?	do-vey pos-so ree-tee-ra-rey eel mee-o ba-ga-leo
It's on Carousel (2), which is down there to the left.	E' al nastro bagagli (2), che è quello in fondo sulla destra.	ey al na-stro ba-ga-lee (2), ke ey kwel-lo een fon-do sul-la deh-stra
Where's a bathroom, please?	Dov'è il bagno per piacere?	dov-ay el ba-neo per pea-che-rey
Where can I catch (a taxi)?	Dove posso prendere un taxi?	do-veh pos-so pr-n-de-rey un taxi
Is there (a shuttle) to the city?	C'è una navetta per la città?	chi una na-vit-ta per la cit-tà
I need to transfer to another flight.	Devo prendere un volo di collegamento.	di-vo pren-di-rey un vo-lo dee kol-le-ga-min-to
We need to find the (railway station).	Dobbiamo trovare la stazione dei treni.	dob-bea-mo tro-va-rey la sta-zio-ney die tre-nee
I have no hotel reservation for tonight.	Non son prenotato in nessun albergo per questa notte.	non sono pr-no-ta-to een nes-sun al-ber-go per kwe-sta not-tey
Can you suggest somewhere nearby, please?	Può suggerirmi qualcosa qui vicino, per piacere?	può sug-ge-re-rmee kwal co-sa kwi vee-cee-no per pea-che-rey

Travel Essentials

> Travel Essentials

While you're in Italy, some basic phrases will make getting around and enjoying yourself much easier.

In this chapter, and on the second CD, we'll start at the airport, find our way around the hotel, move out to the streets, ride public transportation, and rent a car. Then we'll ask for directions, take care of the children, and learn how to get medical help.

At the airport

First, here are a few important words and phrases to get you started:

ENGLISH	ITALIAN	PRONUNCIATION
the airport	l'aereoporto	l aero-por-to
the baggage claim	zona ritiro bagagli	zona ree-tee-ro ba-ga-lee
check in	check-in	check-in
the hotel	l'hotel	l-otel
a hotel room	una stanza di albergo	oona stan-za dee al-ber-go
the metro	la metropolitana	la metro-polee-ta-nah
the railway station	la stazione dei treni	la sta-zeo-ney d-hey tre-nee
a rental car	una macchina in affitto	oona mak-ke-nay een af-fit-to
a restaurant	un ristorante	oon ris-to-ran-tey
a taxi	un taxi	oon taxi
the tour desk	ufficio viaggi	uf-fi-ceo vee-a-cee

BONUS Conversations include finding your luggage, getting a connecting flight, renting a car, and taking a taxi.

Here are a few helpful phrases you may need to use once you're out of the airport and looking for transport:

Where's the bus stop?	Dov'è la fermata del bus?	do-vey ey lah fer-ma-tah dhel bus
How often do the buses come past here?	Quanto spesso passa il bus?	kwan-tou spes-soh pas-sah eel bus
Where do we catch a shuttle?	Dove possiamo prendere la navetta?	doh-vey pos-sea-moh pren-de-rey lah nah-vet-ta
How do we get into the city?	Come si arriva in città?	ko-meh see ar-ree-vah een chet-tah
Is there a metro station nearby?	C'è una stazione della metropolitana vicino?	che oonah stha-zeo-neh dell-ah metro-pol-eetana vee-cee-noh
Where can I get a rental car?	Dove posso noleggiare una macchina?	do-veh pos-soh no-lig-gea-re oona mak-ki-na
You: **Hello. Can you take us to the Hotel Santa Lucia on the Calle della Misericordia, please?**	Salve. Potete portarci all'Hotel Santa Lucia, Calle della Misericordia?	sal-veh. Po-teh-teh por-tar-cee all otel San-tah Lucia, Kalleh del-lah mee-seree-kor-dea
Taxi driver: **Certainly. Let me take your bags.**	Certamente. Mi lasci prendere il suo bagaglio.	che-rta-men-teh. Mee lashy pren-dhe-rey eel suo ba-ga-leo
You: **What will the fare be, approximately?**	Quanto è la tariffa più o meno?	kwan-to ey lah tare-ffa pew o meh-no
Taxi driver: **It'll be around €15.**	Attorno ai €15.	at-tor-no ahi €15

At the hotel

Once you've cleared the airport and found transport, there's only one step left between you and a long, cool drink – you need to check into your accommodation.

Once you've checked in, your next thought may be to get something to eat or drink. But often after a flight or train trip, the last thing you want is to head back out to the streets and find a restaurant. Room service is the perfect solution.

BONUS Conversations include checking into a hotel and ordering room service.

After a meal, sightseeing is next on the list. Organized tours can be a great way to see the main attractions and learn more about the place you're staying in.

BONUS Conversations include talking to a tour desk operator.

Traveling in regional areas

If you're venturing beyond the city you arrived in and traveling within the country by train, bus, boat, or rental car, knowing some of the language is even more important. In the regional areas of Italy, there are often not many people who speak English, but don't worry! We have all the phrases you need to get from A to B.

BONUS Conversations include arranging transport at the railway station and the ferry terminal.

Renting a car or motorbike

Sometimes it's nice to be independent of public transport, especially if you're travelling somewhere that can't be easily reached by train or bus. The driving in Italy may be rather more hectic than you're used to, but renting a car can be a good option in the countryside. Motorcycles are also good outside the cities, if your luggage isn't too heavy.

Remember, the Italians drive on the right-hand side of the road, and you must carry your passport and driver's license, car ownership papers, and proof of third-party insurance at all times. You'll also need an international insurance certificate, and you must drive with headlights on outside urban areas.

BONUS Conversations include renting a car.

Traveling with kids

Traveling with children can bring a whole new dimension to your journey. It's true children can get bored easily, but they're generally also delighted with the smallest of pleasures. Below are some words and phrases that may help you out of a tricky spot when traveling with kids.

We're traveling with young children.	Siamo viaggiando con i nostri bambini.	see-amo vee-aggee-an-doh kon ee no-stree bam-bee-nee
We have a small baby.	Abbiamo un bambino piccolo.	ab-be-amo oon bam-bee-no peek-olo
a crib	un lettino	oon let-tee-noh
a quiet room	una stanza tranquilla	oona stan-za tran-kwi-lla
a family unit	una famiglia unita	oona fa-mee-liah unee-tah
laundry facilities	lavanderia	lav-and-er-ei
a children's menu	un menu bambini	oon menu bam-bee-nee
a highchair	un seggiolone	oon seg-geo-lo-neh
a child's car seat	un seggiolino per l'auto	oon seg-geo-lee-noh per l au-toh
a play area	un parco giochi	oon par-ko gio-kee
the zoo	lo zoo	loh zo

BONUS Conversations include booking rooms, arranging food, and planning tours for kids and families.

Daily necessities

There are some things that you'll need on a daily basis, so it's vital to know how to ask about them. Here are some phrases you may need:

an internet café	un internet cafè	oon internet cafè
a supermarket	un supermercato	oon supermer-cah-to
bottled water	acqua in bottiglia	ak-ua een bot-tee-lea
a newspaper	un giornale	oon geor-nha-ley
a phone card	una carta telefonica	oona kar-tah teh-leh-fo-nee-ka
a café	un bar	oon bar
a restaurant	un ristorante	oon ree-sto-ran-tey
a bank	una banca	oona ban-ka
a post office	un ufficio postale	oon ooffee-ceo pos-ta-li
a fax machine	un fax	oon fax
Can you tell me how to find the nearest supermaket, please?	Mi può dire dove posso trovare il supermarket più vicino, per piacere?	mee puoh dee-rey do-veh pos-soh tro-vah-rey eel supermarket pew vee-cee-no per pea-che-rey
Where can I check my email?	Dove posso controllare le mie email?	do-veh pos-so kon-trol-la-rey leh mei email
Is there an internet café nearby?	C'è un internet cafè qui vicino?	che oon internet cafè kwe vee-cee-no
Do you have wireless internet?	Avete wireless internet?	ave-teh wireless internet
Where can I get some bottled water?	Dove posso comperare acqua in bottiglia?	do-veh pos-soh kom-per-arey ak-ua een bot-tee-lea
Is there a café within walking distance?	C'è un bar raggiungibile a piedi?	che oon bar raggeun-gee-bee-lee ah pee-a-dee
Where can I buy a newspaper?	Dove posso comperare un giornale?	do-veh pos-soh kom-per-arey oon gior-na-leh
I'd like to top up my phone card, please.	Vorrei ricaricare la mia carta telefonica, grazie.	vor-rey ree-ka-ree-ka-rey lah mea kar-tah teh-leh-fo-nee-ka, gra-zea
I need to arrange a telegraphic bank transfer.	Devo fare un bonifico.	deh-voh fa-reh oon bon-ee-fee-ko
Can I send a fax from here?	Posso spedire un fax da qui?	poss-oh speh-dee-rey oon fax dah kwee
Can you direct me to the nearest post office, please?	Mi potrebbe indicare l'ufficio postale più vicino, grazie?	mee poh-tre-bey en-dee-ka-rey l uffe-ceo postal-eh pew vee-cee-noh
Turn left	Gira a sinistra	gee-rah ay see-nee-strah
To the right	Alla destra	allah deh-strah
Straight ahead	Diritto	dee-reet-toh
Around the corner	Dietro l'angolo	dee-atroh l an-go-loh
At the roundabout	Alla rotonda	allah roh-ton-dah
Past the traffic lights	Dopo il semaforo	doh-poh eel sem-afo-roh
Keep going	Continua ad andare avanti	con-tee-nua ahd an-da-rey ava-ntee
Next to	Vicino a	vee-cee-noh ah
Before	Prima	pree-mah
After	Dopo	doh-poh

There may also be times when you or someone you're traveling with needs medical care. Some of the first words you'll want to know are:

a doctor	un dottore	oon dot-to-rey
an ambulance	una ambulanza	oona am-bulan-zah
first aid	primo soccorso	pree-mo sok-kor-soh
a hospital	un ospedale	oon os-peh-dhal-eh
the emergency room	pronto soccorso	pronto soc-cor-soh
a pharmacy (drugstore)	una farmacia	oona phar-ma-chea
travel insurance	assicurazione per un viaggio	assee-kura-zeo-nee per oon veag-geo
Help!	Aiuto!	aee-uto

 BONUS Conversations include arranging medical attention, obtaining prescriptions, getting help for injuries or illness, and calling an ambulance.

Other useful words are:

cold	freddo	frid-do
hot	caldo	kal-do
it hurts	fa male	fah mah-leh
a fever	febbre	feh-br-eh
sore	dolente	dhol-lin-teh
broken	rotto	rot-to
bleeding	sanguinare	san-ghue-nah-rey
nauseous	nausea	nahu-si-ah
cramps	crampi	kram-pee
vomiting	vomitare	vou-mee-tah-rey
a cough	uno starnuto	oono strar-noo-toh
breathing	respirare	reh-spee-rah-reh
diarrhea	diarrea	deir-rhea
a cold	un raffreddore	oon raf-frid-doh-reh
the flu	l'influenza	l' een-flu-n-zah
a rash	un arrossamento	oon ar-roh-sah-men-toh
a burn	una bruciatura	oona bru-chea-tu-rah
a blister	una bolla	oona bhol-lah
a cut	un taglio	oon tah-leo

Dining Out

> Dining Out

A key part of travel is food – whether you eat in or dine out, get a light snack, or order a sumptuous restaurant meal. Here we list words and phrases you will need in cafés and restaurants, in bars, and at markets and street stalls. We'll look at phrases you'll need if you want to buy picnic food or supplies for a camping trip. Then we'll ask about the local cuisine and wines, go to a fast-food outlet, and order vegetarian meals and food for allergy-sufferers.

At the café or restaurant

Below are a few key words and phrases to get you started.

ENGLISH	ITALIAN	PRONUNCIATION
a café	un bar	oon bar
a restaurant	un ristorante	oon ree-sto-ran-teh
a reservation	una prenotazione	oona pre-no-ta-zeo-neh
a meal	un pasto	oon pas-toh
breakfast	colazione	ko-la-zeo-neh
lunch	pranzo	pran-zoh
dinner	cena	che-nah
the menu	il menu	eel menu
a table for two	un tavolo per due	oon tav-oloh per dua
a table for four	un tavolo per quattro	oon tav-oloh per kwat-troh
my/our order	il mio/nostro ordine	eel meo/nos-troh ordee-neh
sparkling water	acqua gasata	ak-ua gas-atah
still water	acqua naturale	ak-ua natur-al-eh
tap water	acqua di rubinetto	ak-wa dee rubee-net-toh
juice	succo	suk-ko
wine	vino	vee-noh
beer	birra	beer-rah
coffee	caffè	kaf-feh
You: Hi. We're here for lunch.	Salve. Siamo qua per pranzo.	sal-veh. See-amo kwa per pran-zo
Restaurant server: Take a seat.	Sedetevi.	seh-deh-teh-vee
I'll bring you some menus.	Vi porto il menu.	vee por-toh eel menu
You: Thank you.	Grazie.	gra-zea

 BONUS Conversations include ordering drinks and sampling wine.

The menu

Regional menu options vary widely, but there are a few terms that will be useful to you throughout Italy.

appetizer	antipasto	antee-pas-toh
avocado	avocado	avocado
beans	fagioli	fah-geo-lee
beef	carne di bovino	kar-neh dee boh-vee-noh
bread	pane	pah-neh
cake of the day	torta del giorno	tor-tah dhel geor-noh
cheese	formaggio	for-mag-geeo
cheese menu	menu dei formaggi	menu d-hey for-mag-gee

chocolate mousse	mousse al cioccolato	muss ahl cheo-kko-la-toh
crepes	crepes	crepes
fish	pesce	peh-sch-eh
lamb	agnello	anee-ehllo
lettuce	lattuga	lat-thu-gah
entrée	primo	pree-mo
meat	carne	kar-neh
onions	cipolle	che-poh-ll-eh
peppers	pepe	peh-peh
pork	maiale	ma-he-aleh
potatoes	patate	pah-tah-teh
seafood	frutti di mare	frut-tee dee ma-rey
soup	minestra	me-neh-stra
soup of the day	minestra del giorno	me-neh-strah dhel geor-noh
tart	crostata	kros-sta-tah
veal	vitello	vee-tell-oh
vegetables	verdure	ver-dhu-reh

 BONUS Conversations include ordering meals and dessert, and paying the bill (check).

At the bar

Here are a few words and phrases you'll need to know when you visit an Italian bar for drinks or a quick bar meal:

bar	bar	bar
bistro	taverna	ta-veh-rnah
order	ordine	or-dee-neh
the smoking area	area fumatori	ah-reh-ah fu-mah-to-ree
beer	birra	beer-rah
draft beer	birra alla spina	beer-rah allah spee-nah
a bottle of beer	una bottiglia di birra	oona bot-tee-leeah dee beer-rah
wine	vino	vee-noh
a glass of wine	un bicchiere di vino	oon beek-ke-erey dee vee-noh
a bottle of wine	una bottiglia di vino	oona bot-tee-leah dee vee-noh
orange juice	succo d'arancia	suk-koh dee ah-rhan-chea
lemonade	limonata	le-mon-ah-tah
coke	coca cola	koka kolah
a snack	uno snack	oono snack
a burger	un hamburger	oon ham-burger
fries	patatine	patha-tee-neh
a pizza	una pizza	oona peez-za

BONUS Conversations include ordering beers and other drinks, and negotiating a smoking or non-smoking venue.

At the market

Italy is justifiably famous for its markets and outdoor eating; the food is usually wonderfully fresh and seasonal, and the prices are good. Here is a short exchange that contains some phrases you might need:

You: Excuse me, could I taste some cheese, please?	Mi scusi, potrei assaggiare del formaggio, per piacere?	mee sku-see, poh-tre-e ass-agg-earey dhel for-mag-geeo, per pea-che rey
The caciotta first, and then the gorgonzola?	Prima la caciotta e poi il gorgonzola?	pree-mah lah kaceot-tah ey poe el gor-gon-zoh-lah
Vendor: Sure. Here's a small piece of each.	Certo. Ecco un assaggio.	cher-toh. Ek-ko oon as-sag-geo
Would you like to try any others before you choose?	Vuole provarne altri prima di decidere?	vuo-e pro-var-ney al-tree an-ko-rah pree-mah dee deh-che-deh-rey
You: Yes. Do you have a soft goat's cheese?	Avete un formaggio morbido di capra?	aveh-teh oon for-mag-geeo mor-bee-doh dee ka-pra
Vendor: Here you are.	Eccolo qua.	ek-ko-lo kwa
You: Wow ... delicious.	Wow ... delizioso.	wow ... dhel-e-zeo-soh
Can I have 100 grams of the caciotta and 100 grams of the goat's cheese, please?	Vorrei 100 grammi della caciotta e 100 grammi del formaggio di capra, grazie?	vor-rey 100 gram-mee dellah ka-ceot-tah ey 100 gram-mee dhel for-mag-geo dee ka-pra, grazea

BONUS Conversations include buying produce.

Tea

You can order tea in most places in Italy. China or black tea is available, generally without milk and with lemon.

tea for one	un te	oon teh
tea for two	due te	due teh
pot of tea	una teiera	oona teh-hee-erah
cup	tazza	ta-zzah
mug	tazzona	taz-zonah
Earl Grey tea	te Earl Grey	teh Earl Grey
breakfast tea	te breakfast	teh breakfast
with milk	con latte	kon latte
with sugar	con zucchero	kon zuk-ke-roh
no milk	senza latte	sen-zah latte
no sugar	senza zucchero	sen-zah zuk-ke-roh
artificial sweetener	dolcificante	dol-cee-fee-kan-teh
with lemon	con limone	kon lee-mo-neh
with honey	con miele	kon mee-eleh
herbal tea	tisana	tee-sa-nah

Coffee

Good quality espresso coffee is to be expected throughout Italy, but don't ask for a 'latte' as you will only receive a cup of milk; it's a *caffellatte* here.

Here's a glossary of some of the types of coffee available. Refer to the CD or DVD for phrases you'll need when ordering the following:

Espresso	a short black espresso
Caffellatte	espresso coffee with steamed milk
Caffè doppio	long, strong black espresso
Caffè americano	long black espresso
Cappuccino	espresso with steamed milk and foam
Caffè freddo	iced coffee

 BONUS Conversations include ordering different styles of coffee.

Outdoors

Whether you're camping in a national park, staying in hostels, or spending a week in a villa, you'll need to buy food to cook and supplies to keep you going. Once again, local markets are a good place to go, though sometimes your only option will be a supermarket or village store.

Here are a few basic words to start with:

bakery	panetteria	pah-neh-tter-eah
basket	cesto	che-sto
bottled water	bottiglia di acqua	botte-lea dee ak-wa
bread	pane	pah-neh
butcher	macellao	mah-chel-lah-eo
butter	burro	burroh
canned goods	cibo in scatola	che-bo en ska-to-lah
cheese	formaggio	for-mag-geeo
dehydrated food	cibo disidratato	che-boh dee-see-dra-ta-toh
fish	pesce	peh-sch-eh
fruit	frutta	frut-tah
groceries	generi alimentary	ge-neh-ree alee-men-ta-ree
local market	mercato di zona	mer-ka-to dee zona
meat	carne	kar-ne
milk	latte	latte
pasta	pasta	pasta
pastry shop	pasticceria	pas-tee-che-rea
shopping cart	carrello	kar-re-llo
supermarket	supermaket	supermarket
vegetables	verdure	ver-du-reh

BONUS Conversations include buying food and navigating your way around the market.

Here are a few more items you may want to buy:

baby food	cibo per neonati	che-bo per neo-nat-ee
baby formula	latte in polvere	latte en pol-veh-rey
canned fish	pesce in scatola	pesh-i en ska-to-la
flour	farina	fa-ree-na
gas cartridge	bombola del gas	bom-bo-la dhel gas
gas cooker	fornelli a gas	for-neh-llee ah gas
lighter	accendino	acch-n-deeno
long-life milk	latte a lunga conservazione	latte ah lun-gah cons-her-va-zeo-neh
matches	cerini	ce-ree-nee
minced meat	carne macinata	kar-neh ma-cee-na-ta
muesli	muesli	muesli
noodles	noodles	noodles
olive oil	olio d'oliva	olio dee olee-vah
portable barbecue	barbecue portatile	barbecue por-ta-tee-leh
rice	riso	ree-so
soup	minestra	mee-neh-strah
steak	bistecca	bee-steh-ka
tomatoes	pomodori	po-moh-doh-ree

Local specialities

One of the highlights of Italian food is the freshness and quality of the local produce, as well as the great variety of regional foods. Depending on where you are, you should be able to track down pizza, pasta, ragù, and local wines in many different guises. Here are some phrases that will help you sample the best each region has to offer:

You: We'd like to try one of the local specialities, please.	Vorremmo provare una delle specialità della zona, grazie.	vor-rem-moh pro-vah-rey oona delleh spech-ea-lee-ta del-la zo-na, grazea
Staff member: This region is well known for its pasta.	Questa zona è rinomata per la pasta.	kwe-sta zo-na ey ree-nom-at-ah per lah pas-tah
You: Oh really? What can you suggest?	Oh, veramente? Cosa mi suggerisce?	oh, veh-rah-men-teh ko-sa mee sug-ger-esceh
Staff member: We have good potato gnocchi. It's very tasty with a rich sauce.	Provi gli gnocchi. Sono molto saporiti con una salsa molto ricca.	pro-vee lee neok-kee so-noh mol-to sah-poh-ree-tee kon unah sal-sa mol-to rek-ka
You: Great. Can I have half a kilo, please?	Posso averne mezzo chilo per piacere?	pos-soh aver-neh mez-zo kee-loh per pea-che-rey

BONUS Conversations include sampling local cuisine and asking for wine recommendations.

Quick bites

If you're looking for a quick, inexpensive meal, there are fast-food and takeout places in almost any town or suburb in Italy, and often the Indian, Asian, and African restaurants offer wonderful meals. Here are some words to help you order:

burger	hamburger	ham-burger
cheeseburger	cheeseburger	chees-burger
double cheeseburger	doppio cheeseburger	doh-ppeo chees-burger
fries	patatine	pa-tah-tee-neh
extra onion	extra di cipolle	extra dee che-pol-leh
pizza	pizza	pizza
chicken curry	pollo al curry	pol-loh hal curry
noodles	noodles	noodles
rice	riso	ree-so
sandwich	sandwich	sandwich
sushi	sushi	sushi
salad	insalata	en-sah-lah-tah
stir-fry	frittura	fret-tu-rah

Allergies and special diets

Being able to order a meal without certain ingredients can be vital if you have food allergies or a special diet. If you require halal or kosher foods, can't eat dairy products, or are allergic to something like peanuts, you'll need to know how to convey your requests clearly. Vegetarians will have quite a few options to choose from, although vegan options may be a little more difficult to find. Here are some basic words and phrases:

vegetarian	vegetariano	veg-et-areano
vegan	vegano	vega-no
vegetarian options	alternative vegetariane	alter-nat-eeve veg-eta-reaney
no meat	niente carne	nee-n-teh car-ney
fish is okay	pesce va bene	peh-sch-ey vah beh-neh
no dairy products	non latticini	non lat-tee-ceenee
no onion or garlic	nè cipolle nè aglio	neh cee-pol-leh neh a-leo
halal foods	cibo halal	cee-boh halal
kosher foods	cibo kosher	cee-boh kosher
sensitive to	sensibile a	sen-see-bee-leh ah
allergic to	allergico a	all-ergee-ko ah
diabetic	diabetico	dea-betee-ko
wheat	grano	gra-no
gluten	glutine	glu-tee-ney
wheat-free	senza grano	sen-za gra-no
gluten-free	senza glutine	sen-za glu-te-ney
dairy-free	senza lattosio	sen-za latto-seo
nuts	noccioline	noc-cheolee-ney
soy milk	latte di soia	latte dee soy-ah

Do you have any vegetarian options?	Avete delle scelte vegetariane?	ave-tey dell-eh sch-eh-ltey veg-eetaree-aney
I don't eat meat.	Non mangio carne.	non man-geo kar-ney
I eat a little fish.	Mangio un pò di pesce.	non man-geo peh-sch-ey
Is this halal/kosher food?	C'è cibo halal/kosher?	che hel cee-boh halal/kosher
I'm diabetic.	Sono diabetico.	so-noh dea-beh-tee-ko
I'm allergic to nuts.	Sono allergico alle noccioline.	so-noh all-er-gee-ko halleh noc-ceo-lee-neh
I'm allergic to shellfish.	Sono allergico ai crostacei.	so-noh all-er-gee-ko haee kro-sta-ch-ey
I'm lactose-intolerant.	Sono intollerante al lattosio.	so-noh en-tol-leh-ran-tey hal latt-oseo
I don't eat dairy products.	Non mangio latticini.	non man-geo lattee-chee-nee
No salt.	Niente sale.	nee-n-tey sa-leh

Entertainment

> Entertainment

And now to the really fun stuff – how to fill your days in Italy!

In this chapter we'll discover the big attractions of a city or region, visit a gallery or museum, find a nightclub or bar, and go shopping. We'll also search out live music and spend an evening at the theater or the movies. For outdoor enthusiasts, we'll learn how to rent bicycles, take part in sporting and adventure activities, and ask about local accommodation so you can stay and enjoy them all!

Let's look first at the big attractions.

ENGLISH	ITALIAN	PRONUNCIATION
bike tour	tour in bicicletta	tour en bee-cee-cl-eh-ta
city tour	tour della città	tour dell-ah cheet-tah
coach trip	tour in Pullman	tour en pull-man
entry fee	costo dell'entrata	kos-to dell hen-trah-ta
gardens	giardini	g-ar-dee-nee
heritage tour	tour ai siti storici	tour hai see-tee sto-ree-cee
line	coda	ko-da
tickets	biglietti	bee-lee-et-tee
waiting time	tempo d'attesa	teh-m-poh dee at-teh-sah
wine tour	tour enologico	tour hen-olo-g-ko
the train station	la stazione dei treni	lah st-haz-eo-ney d-hey tre-nee
the Colosseum	Il Colosseo	El Kol-os-ey-o
the Amalfi Coast	La Costiera Amalfitana	La Kost-e-era Amal-fee-ta-na
the Vatican City	Città del Vaticano	Chee-tah dhel Va-tee-ka-noh
Roman Forum	I Fori Romani	Ee Fo-ree Ro-man-ee
Sistine Chapel	La Cappella Sistina	Lah Kap-pel-lah See-stee-nah
the Pantheon	Il Pantheon	El Pan-teh-on
the Spanish Steps	Scalinata di Trinità dei Monti	Ska-lee-nah-tah dee Tree-nee-tah d-hey Mon-tee
Venetian Canals	I Canali di Venezia	Ee Ka-na-lee dee Veh-nhe-ze-ah
the Dolomites	Le Dolomiti	L-ey Doh-loh-mee-tee

 BONUS Conversations include asking for directions, purchasing tickets, enquiring about opening hours, and taking a tour.

Shopping

There are only so many hours in a day that you can visit attractions, wait in lines, and enjoy the sights. Sometimes a bit of retail therapy is needed to clear the mind! Or you may want to pick up some local specialities to take back with you. Here are a few good phrases to know:

antique store	antiquario	antee-kwa-ree-o
book shop	negozio di libri	nego-zeeo dee lee-bree
boutique	boutique	boutique
clothing store	negozio di abbigliamento	nego-zeo dee ab-be-le-amen-to
department store	grandi magazzini	gran-dee mag-az-zee-nee
gift shop	negozio di articoli da regalo	nego-zeo dee artee-kolee dah re-gha-lo
price	prezzo	prez-zo

sale	sconti	skon-tee
shopping center	centro commerciale	chen-tro kom-mer-che-al-eh
shopping tour	tour di negozi	tour dee nego-zee
souvenirs	souvenirs	souvenirs
textile store	negozio di tessuti	nego-zeo dee tess-utee

 BONUS Conversations include enquiring about shops, finding speciality items, and asking for recommendations.

Educational fun

Galleries and museums offer great insights into the history and culture of a place. Put a few on your list of things to see!

art gallery	galleria d'arte	ghal-le-rea d ar-tey
cultural tour	tour culturale	tour kul-tu-raleh
entry fee	costo dell'entrata	kos-to dell ent-ra-ta
exhibition	esibizione	esee-bee-zeo-neh
information sheet	foglietto informativo	folee-eh-to een-for-mat-eevo
library	biblioteca	bib-leo-te-ka
local history	storia locale	story-ah local-eh
museum	museo	mu-sio
opening hours	orari d'apertura	ora-ree dee ap-eh-rturah
self-guided tour	tour indipendente	tour n-deep-n-den-te
video display	video display	video display

BONUS Conversations include asking about opening hours, entry fees, and directions.

Nightlife

After a hard day enjoying the art and culture of the area, evening is the time to search out some good food and entertainment. Let's explore the local nightlife!

ballet	ballo	bah-lo
cinema	cinema	cinema
classical music	musica classica	muse-ka kla-see-ka
cocktail bar	cocktail bar	cocktail bar
cover charge	coperto	ko-per-toh
dance bar	discoteca	desko-ti-ka
DJ	DJ	DJ
jazz club	jazz club	jazz club
live music	musica dal vivo	mu-see-ka dal vee-vo
nightclub	nightclub	nightclub
opera	opera	opera
theater	teatro	teh-ah-tro

BONUS Conversations include how to find opera, live music or a DJ, and booking tickets to the theater.

Sporting activities

Italy boasts an impressive number of national parks and World Heritage areas, an interesting array of native birds and animals, and a rich tapestry of heritage villages to explore. Back in the cities, most have a spectacular garden or two, and the coastlines are littered with beautiful beaches. In this section we'll look at cycling, sailing, skiing, swimming, white-water rafting, beach walks, golf, and exploring islands and ruins.

adventure activities	avventure	ha-vin-turey
beach	spiaggia	spea-geah
boating	andare in barca	an-darey een bar-ka
camping	camping	camping
clothes optional	vestiti facoltativi	ves-tee-tee fa-kol-ta-tee-vee
coastline	costa	kos-ta
countryside	campagna	kam-pa-nea
cycle paths	piste ciclabili	pee-stey cee-cla-bee-lee
cycling	andare in bici	an-da-rey een bee-cee
danger	pericolo	per-ee-kolo
dinghy	canotto	kan-ot-to
guide	guida	gue-dah
high tide	alta marea	al-ta ma-ri-ah
hiking trails	sentieri	sen-tee-eh-ree
kayaking	fare kayak	fah-reh kayak
low tide	bassa marea	bass-ah ma-ri-ah
national park	parco nazionale	par-ko na-zeo-nah-ley
outdoors	all'aperto	ahll ah-per-to
public garden	giardini pubblici	ge-ar-dee-nee phu-blee-che
rip	strappo	strap-po
safe for swimming	sicuro per nuotare	see-ku-roh per nuo-ta-rey
sailing	navigare	na-vee-ga-rey
skiing	sciare	schee-arey
sunbathing	prendere il sole	pre-nderey el so-leh
swimming	nuotare	nuo-tarey
walking	camminare	kam-mee-na-rey
white-water rafting	rafting	rafting
yacht	yacht	yacht

 BONUS Conversations include renting bicycles or sailboats, finding a local golf course, getting information about local beach walks and swimming conditions, and booking a white-water rafting or ski trip.

Exploring

Regional areas aren't always covered in guidebooks – there's far too much to see and do! So how do you explore areas that interest you? Easy, ask the locals!

castle	castello	kas-teh-lo
ferry	traghetto	tra-ghetto
islands	isole	eeso-ley
jetty	molo	mol-oh
motorbike	moto d'acqua	mo-to dee akwa
ruins	rovine	rovee-neh

BONUS Conversations include booking local accommodation and exploring nearby islands and ruins.

Further Study

If you're planning an extended stay in Italy, your needs will be different from those of someone planning to pass through in a week. For starters, there are more great wines than you can taste in a week, when you have the whole of Tuscany and Abruzzo before you! You'll need time for that! And more importantly, you'll need some more language skills in order to interact with the locals during an extended stay.

In this final chapter, and on the fifth CD, we'll uncover some useful travel tips and shortcuts for travelling through Italy and then look at some extras – business talk; what you'll need to ask for if you want to extend your stay; and a few words you'll need to understand if you're looking to buy a property.

Lastly, we'll look at some grammar-related items, including a run-through of the alphabet, so you can spell out your new address at the post office, and a look at the basic structure of verbs – once you've gotten them under control you'll feel a lot more confident speaking Italian.

But to start, here are a few things it's helpful to know upfront.

- **Culture** – Italy has a stand-out culture of its own, reflected in the people as well as their food, art, and customs. Immigrant cultures from Africa have also added spice to the traditional Italian way of life. The family unit, both nuclear and extended, is the most important structure in Italian society and culture.
- **Style** – It's all true: style is key in Italy. A good personal image – *la bella figura* – is the measuring stick used to judge people within the first few moments of meeting, taking into account their appearance, dress, and manner.
- **Etiquette** – When you meet someone new or a passing acquaintance, a handshake is best. Save the kissing (once on each cheek, leaning right) for people you know well and greet people as *Signore, Signora,* or *Signorina* until you're on familiar terms with them; only then should you use first names. Greet everyone as you enter a room, and in a business setting say *buon giorno* or *buona sera* before taking a seat, ordering a drink, or joining a conversation.
- **Tipping** – In restaurants, a service charge is included in the check. Italians don't usually leave tips.

Now to some specifics.

Immigration

People choose extended stays in Italy for many reasons. One of the first things you'll need to do after you've decided to extend your stay is to check your immigration requirements. You'll probably need to renew your visa at least. Check with your home embassy or consulate, or ask someone local to point you in the right direction.

ENGLISH	ITALIAN	PRONUNCIATION
You: **Good morning. I want to know if my visa needs renewing.**	Buongiorno. Vorrei sapere se il mio visto deve essere rinnovato.	buon-geor-no. Vor-rey sap-erey seh eel meo vee-stoh de-veh s-serey ree-no-va-to
Embassy staff member: **Sure. How long have you been in Italy?**	Certo. Per quanto siete stati in Italia?	cher-to. Per kwan-to see-eh-teh sta-tee een Eetalea
You: **We arrived on June 20, so we've been here for two and a half months.**	Siamo arrivati il 20 di Giugno, quindi siamo qui da 2 mesi e mezzo.	see-amo r-re-vate eel 20 dee geu-neo. Kwin-dee see-amo kwee da 2 meh-see e mez-zoh
Embassy staff member: **Okay. If you plan to stay more than ninety days, you'll need a *permesso di soggiorno.***	Okay. Se volete stare quà più di 90 giorni, avete bisogno del 'permesso di soggiorno'.	okay. Seh voh-leh-teh sta-rey kwa pew de 90 geor-nee ave-tey bee-so-neo dhel per-mess-oh dee sog-georno
You: **What documents do I need to provide? How much does it cost?**	Che documenti devo portare? Quanto costa?	ke doh-ku-men-tee de-vo port-arey. Kwan-to kos-ta
Embassy staff member: **The *permesso* is €149.**	Costa €149.	kos-ta €149

You will need your passport and four passport photos.	Servono ilvostro passaporto e quattro foto per passaporto.	ser-voh-no eel vos-tro pass-ap-orto e kwat-tro pho-to per pass-apor-to
You'll need to explain why you want to stay.	Dovrete indicare perchè volete restare.	do-vreh-teh en-dee-ka-rey per-ke vo-leh-teh reh-stah-rey
You'll also need a return ticket and be able to show you can support yourself during your stay.	Dovrete anche avere un biglietto aereo di ritorno e dimostrare di essere in grado di potervi mantenere.	doh-vreh-teh an-ke ave-rey oon bee-lee-et-to ai-rio dee ree-thor-no ey dee-mos-tr-arey dee s-serey een gra-doh dee pot-eh-rvee man-ten-erey

Renting accommodation

Chances are you'll need to look for more permanent accommodation, perhaps rent an apartment, get utilities signed up, and maybe even join the library. Here are a few handy phrases.

You: **Good morning. We'd like to view the apartment you advertised on the Via della Scala.**	Buongiorno. Vorremmo vedere l'appartamento pubblicizzato in Via della Scala da voi.	buon-georno. Voh-reh-moh veh-deh-rey l ap-par-tam-eh-nto pu-bleech-ezato da voi een vea dell-ah Ska-la da voi
Rental agent: **Ah yes, of course. Just a few questions first.**	Ah, si. Prima solo alcune domande.	ah, see. Pre-ma so-lo al-ku-nee dom-an-dee
Do you live here in Italy now?	Vivete in Italia adesso?	vee-veh-tey een Eeta-lea adh-s-so
You: **Yes, we arrived in April and have both found work here, so we're staying. Our visas have been extended for six months.**	Si. Siamo arrivati entrambi in Aprile e abbiamo trovato lavoro, per cui restiamo. I nostri visti sono stati estesi per sei mesi.	see. Sea-mo r-re-va-tee n-tram-bee een April-e ey ab-bea-mo tr-vah-to lav-oro per kwee res-tea-mo. Ee nos-tre ves-tee so-noh sta-tee s-teh-see per sei meh-see
Rental agent: **Do you have references?**	Avete delle referenze?	ave-tey dell-eh referen-zey
You: **Yes, two phone referees, and I have a letter from my employer to confirm my income.**	Si. Due referenze telefoniche e io ho una lettera del mio datore di lavoro che conferma il mio salario.	see. Dui referen-zey teh-leh-phonee-ke ey ee-o ho oona letter-ah dhel meo dat-ore a dee lah-voh-ro ke kon-fer-mah eel meo sal-areo
Rental agent: **Good. We require four weeks' rent in advance.**	Bene. Noi vogliamo quattro settimane di affitto anticipato.	beh-ney. Noee vo-lea-mo kwat-tro settee-man-eh dee af-feet-toh an-tee-cee-patoh
Shall I meet you at the apartment tomorrow at 10am?	Ci vediamo domani alle 10 di mattina davanti all'appartamento?	cee veh-deea-moh do-man-ee alle 10 di-matt-eena dah-van-tee ahll apharta-men-to
You: **That would be great. Thank you.**	Sarebbe perfetto. Grazie.	Sareb-beh per-fet-to. Gra-zea

Connecting the electricity

You: Good morning. Is that the power company?	Buongiorno. Parlo con l'azienda dell'elettricità?	buon geor-no. Par-loh kon l azee-n-dah dell elett-ree-cee-tah
Staff member: Yes, madam. How can I help you?	Si signora, come la posso aiutare?	see se-neo-rah ko-meh lah poss-oh aeu-tah-rey
You: We've signed up to rent a house in Naples and we need to arrange an electricity account with you.	Abbiamo affittato una casa in Napoli e dobbiamo fare un allacciamento elettrico con voi.	ab-beamo af-fee-tah-to oona ka-sa een Na-pol-ee ei doh-beamoh fah-rey oon all-acchea-men-toh l-et-tree-ko kon voee
Staff member: Okay. You'll need to come in to the office.	Okay. Dovete venire nell'ufficio.	okay. Doh-veh-tey veh-nee-ree nell uf-fee-ceo.
Bring your birth certificate and passport, a bank deposit form and an account from another company that confirms your address.	Portate il vostro certificato e il pasaporto, un bollettino di un deposito bancario e un acconto da un'altra società che confermi il vostro indirizzo.	por-tah-tey eel vos-tro chertee-fee-ka-to ey eel pass-aporto, oon boll-ettee-no dee oon deposit-oh bank-areo ey oon ak-kon-to dah oon al-trah so-che-eh-ta ke-con-fer-mee eel vos-tro een-dee-reez-zo
You: That's a lot of papers.	Sono tanti documenti.	so-noh tan-tee document-ee
Are they all necessary?	Sono tutti necessary?	so-noh tut-tee ne-chess-aree
Staff member: Oh yes. We may require other documents as well.	Oh certo. Potremmo aver bisogno anche di altri documenti.	oh che-rto. Pot-rem-moh avere bee-so-neo an-ke dee al-tree document-ee
You: Okay. Do I need to make an appointment?	Okay. Devo prendere un appuntamento?	okay. Devoh pren-deh-rey oon ap-poon-ta-men-toh
Staff member: No. We have staff available most of the time.	No. C'è quasi sempre del personale disponibile.	no. Che kwa-see sem-prey dhel per-so-nah-le dee-spo-nee-bee-lee

Joining the library

You: Hello. We'd like to join the library.	Salve. Vorremmo diventare membri della biblioteca.	sal-veh. Vor-rem-moh dee-ven-tarey mem-bree dell-ah be-bleo-te-ka
Staff member: Do you live here in Rome?	Vivete qui a Roma?	vee-veh-teh kwee ah Ro-mah
You: Yes, we live in zona Tuscalana. We're renting an apartment there.	Si. Viviamo nella zona Tuscolana. Affittiamo un appartamento là.	see, vee-vee-amo nell-ah zo-na Tusko-lan-ah. Af-fee-te-amo oon appar-ta-men-to lah
Staff member: Okay. We'll need to see some proof of your address, please.	Okay. Abbiamo bisogno di qualche prova del vostro indirizzo, grazie.	okay. Ab-bea-mo bee-so-neo dee kwal-ke proh-va del vos-tro in-dee-rizz-oh, gra-zea.
And you'll need to fill out this application form.	E poi dovreste riempire questo modulo.	E poi doh-vres-te ree-eh-pee-rey kwe-sto mod-ulo.
Just drop it back in next time you're passing.	Riportatelo quando ripassate.	ree-por-ta-teh-lo kwan-do ree-pass-atey
You: How long does it take to process the application?	Quando ci si mette a elaborare la domanda?	kwan-do che see met-tey ah l-lab-orarey lah do-man-dah
Staff member: Your library cards will be mailed to you within a week of your application being received.	Le vostre tessere della biblioteca saranno spediti entro una settimana dal momento in cui la domanda sarà ricevuta.	leh vos-tre tess-erey dell-ah bee-bleo-te-ka sarah-no spe-dee-tee ent-ro oona settee-man-ah dhal mom-n-to een kwe la do-man-dah sa-rah ree-chee-vu-ta
Feel free to have a look around today.	Sentitevi liberi di dare un'occhiata intorno.	sen-tee-teh-vee lee-beh-ri dee da-reh oon okkea-ta en-thor-no
Books are issued for four weeks.	I libri saranno pubblicati entro quattro settimane.	ee lee-bree sarah-no puh-blee-katee entro la pros-see-mah set-tee-ma-nah

Buying property

You never know, maybe you'll fall head over heels for the Italian way of life and decide to buy a property in Italy. That idyllic apartment overlooking the Ligurian coast could be the one. Or it could be a pretty villa overlooking the river in Umbria that has you calling your bank manager!

Just be wary and move slowly, as there's a mountain of paperwork and bureaucracy to wade through before you can take ownership. There are only a few English-speaking agencies in Italy that can help you with the purchasing, so you'll need to make sure you understand what's going on around you.

Here are a few terms you'll need to know:

appraiser	perito	per-ee-to
completion	completamento	kom-pleh-tah-men-to
contract	contratto	kon-trat-to
cooling-off period	periodo di riflessione	per-eodoh dee ree-fles-seoney
deposit	deposito	deposit-oh
documents	documenti	document-ee
financial adviser	consulente finanziario	kon-sul-n-teh fee-nan-zea-reo
lawyer	avvocato	av-vo-ka-toh
notary	notaio	not-ha-eo
offer	offerta	off-er-tah
planning office	ufficio catastale	uff-ee-ceo kat-asta-ley
purchaser	compratore	kom-pra-torey
real estate agent	agenzia immobiliare	ag-n-zea m-mobee-leare
services	servizi	ser-vee-zee
sewage	acqeu di scolo	ak-we dee sko-lo
surveyor	perito	per-ee-to
translator	traduttore	tra-dut-orey
utilities	servizi di pubblica utilità	ser-vee-zee dee pub-blee-ka oot-eel-eeta
vendor	venditore	ven-dee-tore

Extended business stays

If you're staying in Italy for an extended period of time because of work or business commitments, rather than for pleasure, some of the words and phrases you'll need have been included earlier in this section. However, there are a number of other terms that will be useful if you require access to online facilities, business finance, local body resources, and so on.

appointment	appuntamento	ap-oon-tam-n-to
bank	banca	bank-ah
broadband connection	connessione broadband	kon-ness-eo-ney broadband
copying services	copisteria	cop-eest-eh-reea
courier	corriere	kor-ree-erey
fax machine	fax	fax
finance company	società finanziaria	so-cee-eh-ta fee-nan-zea-rea
internet provider	internet provider	internet provider
interpreter	interprete	een-ter-pre-teh
local council offices	uffici comunali	uf-fee-cee kom-oona-lee
meeting	riounione	ree-oo-nee-oney
meeting room	stanza delle riunioni	stan-zah dell-eh reu-neo-nee
mobile phone company	società di telefonia mobile	socee-eh-ta dee telephon-ea mobee-leh
planning officer	incaricato della pianificazione	een-karee-cat-oh dell-ah peanee-fee-kazeoney
post office	posta	pos-ta
resource planning	pianificazione delle risorse	peanee-fee-caz-eeoney dell-eh ree-sor-sey
telephone conference	conferenza telefonica	con-fer-n-za tel-f-on-eeka
wireless hotspot	hotspot wireless	hotspot wireless

Studying in Italy

Italy is a popular destination for overseas students and student exchanges. Here are a few phrases you'll need as a student:

You: I'm new here.	Sono nuovo di qui.	so-noh nuo-vo dee kwee
I'm an overseas student.	Sono uno studente straniero.	so-noh oono stu-deh-ntey stra-nee-he-ro
Where do I go first?	Dove devo andare come prima cosa?	do-veh de-vo an-da-rey ko-me pre-ma ko-sa
Staff member: Welcome! You need to go to the enrolment office first.	Benvenuto. Devi prima andare all'ufficio iscrizioni.	ben-ven-uto. De-vee pre-ma an-dah-rey all uffe-ceo is-kree-seon-ee
Make sure you have all your details with you.	Assicurati di avere tutti i tuoi dettagli con te.	assee-kurat-ee de eave-rey tut-tee ee touee det-ta-lee kon te
What are you here to study?	Che cosa studierai?	ke ko-sah stu-dee-eraee
You: I'm doing a six-month course in art history.	Faccio un corso di sei mesi in Soria dell'arte.	fa-ceo oon kor-so dee sei me-si sto-rea dell arteh
It's very exciting to be doing it here in Rome!	Sono molto felice di essere qui a Roma.	so-noh mol-to kon-ten-to dee s-serey kwee ah Ro-mah
Staff member: Yes, you've come to the right city.	Si. Sei venuto nella città giusta.	see. Sei veh-nuh-to nell-ah cet-tah geu-sta
Make sure you visit the Borghese Gallery and Museum whenever you get the chance, as well the National Gallery of Modern Art.	Non perderti il museo e la galleria Borghese e anche la galleria di arte moderna.	non per-dher-tee eel mus-eh-eo ey lah gal-eh-rea Bor-ghe-sey ey an-ke lah gal-ler-ea dee ar-teh mod-r-na
You: I will. Thank you.	Di sicuro. Grazie.	dee see-ku-ro. Gra-zea
You: Excuse me, where can I get these textbooks?	Mi scusi. Dove posso trovare questi libri di testo?	mee sku-see. Do-veh poss-oh tro-va-rey kwe-stee lee-bre dee tes-to
There are no bookshops suggested on the course sheet.	Non ci sono negozi di libri indicati sui fogli del corso.	non cee sono ne-goh-zee dee lee-bree een-dee-ka-tee suee fo-lee dhel kor-soh
Staff member: The university bookshop is on the far side of the social sciences faculty.	Il negozio di libri della facoltà è al fondo dell'isolato della scienze sociali.	eel negoz-eo dee lee-bree dell-ah fak-ol-tah ey al-fon-do dell eso-la-to dell-eh scien-zey so-chea-lee
It will have most of the textbooks listed. Otherwise, try the big bookstore on the via de' Neri.	Ha la maggior parte dei testi indicati. Altrimenti prova il grande negozio di libri su via de' Neri.	ha lah maggeor par-teh deh-ee test-ee en-dee-ka-tee. Altre-men-tee pro-vah eel grand-ey negoz-eo dee lee-bree suh vea de' Neh-ree
You: Does it have English language books?	Ha dei libri in testo inglese?	ha deh-ee lee-bree een test-oh een-gli-si
Staff member: Yes, it specializes in them. It has a great range of books.	Si. E' specializzato. Ne ha una grande varietà.	see. Ey spe-chea-lez-za-to. Neh ha oona gran-dee varee-et-ah

The alphabet

You'll often need to spell out your name, address, or other information to people while you're abroad, and as well as having fewer letters than the English alphabet, many letters in the Italian alphabet are pronounced differently. Here's how to say the alphabet in Italian:

a	a	ah
b	bi	bee
c	ci	chee
d	di	dee
e	e	eh
f	effe	f-feh
g	gi	gee
h	acca	ak-ka
i	i	e
l	elle	el-leh
m	emme	m-meh
n	enne	n-neh
o	o	oh
p	pi	pee
q	cu	ku
r	erre	eh-reh
s	ese	s-seh
t	ti	tee
u	u	uh
v	vu	veu
z	zeta	zi-ta

There are also several extra letter combinations that were covered in the first chapter.

A little more about verbs

When you're learning a new language, verbs can be the most confusing part. Like most European languages, Italian uses a very regular verb structure, although there are exceptions.

The 'regular' verbs, as they are called, follow one of three simple patterns depending on the ending of the base verb, AKA the 'infinitive'. The three regular verb endings are *-are*, *-ere*, and *-ire* – as in *parlare* (to speak), *battere* (to hit), and *capire* (to understand), for example. In each case, to use the verb in a sentence you need to remove the ending and replace it with an ending that matches the gender, tense, and number you're speaking about. For the verb *parlare* and all other regular verbs that end in *-are*, present-tense forms are as follows:

I speak	take off the *are* and add *o*	*io parlo*
You speak (informal singular)	take off the *are* and add *i*	*tu parli*
You speak (formal singular)	take off the *are* and add *a*	*Lei parla*
He/she speaks	take off the *are* and add *a*	*lui/lei parla*
We speak	take off the *are* and add *iamo*	*noi parliamo*
You speak (informal plural)	take off the *are* and add *ate*	*voi parlate*
You speak (formal plural)	take off the *are* and add *ano*	*essi parlano*
They speak	take off the *are* and add *ano*	*loro parlano*

Here is the structure for regular *-ere* verbs such as *battere* (to hit):

I hit	take off the *ere* and add *o*	*io batto*
You hit (informal singular)	take off the *ere* and add *i*	*tu batti*
You hit (formal singular)	take off the *ere* and add *e*	*Lei batte*
He/she hits	take off the *ere* and add *e*	*lui/lei batte*
We hit	take off the *ere* and add *iamo*	*noi battiamo*
You hit (informal plural)	take off the *ere* and add *ete*	*voi battete*
You hit (formal plural)	take off the *ere* and add *ono*	*essi battono*
They hit	take off the *ere* and add *ono*	*loro battono*

Here is the structure for regular *-ire* verbs such as *capire* (to understand):

I understand	take off the *ire* and add *isco*	*io capisco*
You understand (informal singular)	take off the *ire* and add *isci*	*tu capisci*
You understand (formal singular)	take off the *ire* and add *isce*	*Lei capisce*
He/she understands	take off the *ire* and add *isce*	*lui/lei capisce*
We understand	take off the *ire* and add *iamo*	*noi capiamo*
You understand (informal plural)	take off the *ire* and add *ite*	*voi capite*
You understand (formal plural)	take off the *ire* and add *iscono*	*essi capiscono*
They understand	take off the *ire* and add *iscono*	*loro capiscono*

In the past tense, things are even easier. You simply use the verb *avere* (to have) before the regular verb's unchanging 'past participle' form – so once you've learned the different forms of *avere,* you only have to know how to construct a past participle. For *parlare* and other regular *-are* verbs, you make the past participle simply by replacing the *-are* ending with *-ato,* as in *parlato.* For *-ere* verbs, you just remove the *-ere* and replace it with *-uto*: so *battere* becomes *battuto.* For *-ire* verbs, you replace the *-ire* ending with *-ito*: *capire,* for example, becomes *capito.*

The all-important forms of *avere* are as follows:

I have	*io ho*
You have (informal singular)	*tu hai*
You have (formal singular)	*Lei ha*
He/she has	*lui/lei ha*
We have	*noi abbiamo*
You have (informal plural)	*voi avete*
You have (formal plural)	*essi hanno*
They have	*loro hanno*

So, these are the past-tense forms of *parlare*:

I spoke	use *ho* followed by *parlato*	*io ho parlato*
You spoke (informal singular)	use *hai* followed by *parlato*	*tu hai parlato*
You spoke (formal singular)	use *ha* followed by *parlato*	*Lei ha parlato*
He/she spoke	use *ha* followed by *parlato*	*lui/lei ha parlato*
We spoke	use *abbiamo* followed by *parlato*	*noi abbiamo parlato*
You spoke (informal plural)	use *avete* followed by *parlato*	*voi avete parlato*
You spoke (formal plural)	use *hanno* followed by *parlato*	*essi hanno parlato*
They spoke	use *hanno* followed by *parlato*	*loro hanno parlato*

Similarly, the past-tense forms of *battere* are:

I hit	*io ho battuto*
You hit (informal singular)	*tu hai battuto*
You hit (formal singular)	*Lei ha battuto*
He/she hit	*lui/lei ha battuto*
We hit	*noi abbiamo battuto*
You hit (informal plural)	*voi avete battuto*
You hit (formal plural)	*essi hanno battuto*
They hit	*loro hanno battuto*

And the past-tense forms of *capire* are:

I understood	*io ho capito*
You understood (informal singular)	*tu hai capito*
You understood (formal singular)	*Lei ha capito*
He/she understood	*lui/lei ha capito*
We understood	*noi abbiamo capito*
You understood (informal plural)	*voi avete capito*
You understood (formal plural)	*essi hanno capito*
They understood	*loro hanno capito*

To make the future tense of regular verbs, there is a simple rule for each kind of verb ending. For example, the future-tense forms of *parlare* are:

I will speak	take off the *are* and add *erò*	*io parlerò*
You will speak (informal singular)	take off the *are* and add *erai*	*tu parlerai*
You will speak (formal singular)	take off the *are* and add *erà*	*Lei parlerà*
He/she will speak	take off the *are* and add *erà*	*lui/lei parlerà*
We will speak	take off the *are* and add *eremo*	*noi parleremo*
You will speak (informal plural)	take off the *are* and add *erete*	*voi parlerete*
You will speak (formal plural)	take off the *are* and add *eranno*	*essi parleranno*
They will speak	take off the *are* and add *eranno*	*loro parleranno*

For the *-ere* verbs, it's the same principle. Here's the future tense of *battere*:

I will hit	take off the *e* and add *ò*	*io batterò*
You will hit (informal singular)	take off the *e* and add *ai*	*tu batterai*
You will hit (formal singular)	take off the *e* and add *à*	*Lei batterà*
He/she will hit	take off the *e* and add *à*	*lui/lei batterà*
We will hit	take off the *e* and add *emo*	*noi batteremo*
You will hit (informal plural)	take off the *e* and add *ete*	*voi batterete*
You will hit (formal plural)	take off the *e* and add *anno*	*essi batteranno*
They will hit	take off the *e* and add *anno*	*loro batteranno*

And here is *capire:*

I will understand	take off the *e* and add *ò*	*io capirò*
You will understand (informal singular)	take off the *e* and add *ai*	*tu capirai*
You will understand (formal singular)	take off the *e* and add *à*	*Lei capirà*
He/she will understand	take off the *e* and add *à*	*lui/lei capirà*
We will understand	take off the *e* and add *emo*	*noi capiremo*
You will understand (informal plural)	take off the *e* and add *ete*	*voi capirete*
You will understand (formal plural)	take off the *e* and add *anno*	*essi capiranno*
They will understand	take off the *e* and add *anno*	*loro capiranno*

Irregular verbs, of which there are many, do not follow these patterns exactly, although they are generally similar. Unfortunately, you just have to learn irregular verbs individually as you need them!

One important trick to know is that Italian speakers don't always use the words 'I', 'you', and so on. So instead of saying *io capisco* (I understand), they might just say *capisco* (understand). You can tell who's being spoken about by the form of the verb.

Just two more useful pieces of information before we finish. First, along with *avere*, the verb *essere* (to be) is important to know as it's used so often. Its present-tense forms are:

I am	*io sono*
You are (informal singular)	*tu sei*
You are (formal singular)	*Lei è*
He/she is	*lui/lei è*
We are	*noi siamo*
You are (informal plural)	*voi siete*
You are (formal plural)	*essi sono*
They are	*loro sono*

Second, there'll be lots of times when you'll need to use a negative statement. You'll be glad to know that it's simple! You just put *non* before the verb – as in:

*Noi **non** mangiamo le banane.*

We don't eat bananas.

And that's where we finish! Armed with all the newfound knowledge you've acquired from this extended learning section of *Language on the Move*, you should have no trouble ordering an espresso coffee and pizza, finding a remote Umbrian winery, or connecting power to your new Tuscan villa. Enjoy your stay in Italy, and *buon viaggio!*